The Sit N Do Nothing Series

The Gotta Have Hamster Workbook

Volume Six of
The Sit 'N' Do Nothing
Hamster Series

Humans All Make Some Time Exploring Relationships

Written By Wendy Proteau

The Sit N Do Nothing Series

Covers designed by: Wendy Proteau

Copyright2009©WendyProteau
All Rights Reserved
TXU001655158

The Sit N Do Nothing Series

The Gotta Have Hamster

Why a hamster? It is the continual engine that spins the wheel in our brain and every moment of every day it's running. At home, shopping, doctor's office, work, in traffic…it never stops! So much passes through it during our daily routine, it's going and going and going (squeak-squeak-squeak) it's spinning.

Advertisers and the retail world know this. They do everything possible to get stuck in your brain and want us to believe in products/services, hoping we buy into it all. Money truly does make the world go round for them.

So how do you feel about the commercial world? Where does your money go? Do you like advertising or could you come up with better? This book is a playful look at it all. It's about how you feel about the ever changing concepts you're sold and the information you see every day. Are you keeping up with the Jones's or are you the Jones's?

We all see advertisements and we all make money…put two and two together, yep, we spend daily!

So many things are out there that we gotta ask, do we truly need this or is it hype that we buy into? I've done it, so I'm sure you have too. Things we buy and later look back and think– why? There are the necessities of food, clothes, medications and our existence is fueled by getting what we need. For some it's hard enough to make ends meet, while others seem to have all the new and exciting gadgets. Advertisers know how to make us want things and they have their hands in every product or service worldwide. They know how to direct ads towards children, teens, men, women, single or married, making us feel a sense of need. Magazines, radio, TV, flyers, personalities, celebrities, movies…it's everywhere!

Where does your money go? I bet you never stopped to look at it all. These are straightforward questions about spending hard earned cash. We have many opinions and I'm sure there are things that frustrate us about it all.

I'm betting you already know the commercials you hate and actually switch channels when they come on. You're tired of the thirty-nine ads you sift through trying to finish the article you started reading in a magazine. Yet some are brilliant and make us laugh. They get stuck in the hamster wheel. Advertising is absolutely everywhere!

How do they come up with those ideas? Some are way out there and some keep us giggling. I view advertising as the dream job; a boardroom of ideas and being paid to be creative. How nice!

So let's just stop for a moment and reflect on it all. Just one rule

"GOTTA BE HONEST!"

So sit back and have fun with it all.

The Sit N Do Nothing Series

The Gotta Have Hamster

Basic facts about _____, and what I buy into!
(First name please)

Today's date is: _____

Last name_____

I live in _____

Born _____ day _____ month _____ year

Born in_____

Time I was born was at_____

Raised in_____

Other places I've lived over the years:
_____
_____
_____

Education level is _____

I went to the following schools-name and year please:
_____
_____
_____

I work as a_____

I have been at my current job _____ years

The Sit N Do Nothing Series

I have worked in my trade _____ years

This book was given to me by _____

In 5 words I would describe who I am as

1_____

2_____

3_____

4_____

5_____

In 5 words I would describe the person who gave me this book as

1_____

2_____

3_____

4_____

5_____

HAVE FUN!

The Sit N Do Nothing Series

THE GOTTA HAVE HAMSTER

1-Lets just see how you manage things. We all work to make money and spend that money. But it starts with earning in order to buy things, so how does it all start for you? Answer the following when it comes to your work life…there are no sometimes or maybe!

I leave work at work and never take it home ____true _____false

I never really stop working its constant ____true _____false

I work more than one full time job ____true _____false

I love my work that's why I do it ____true _____false

I use work as a way to avoid things ____true _____false

Management so I am expected to work more ____true _____false

I put in my 8 hours and poof I'm free ____true _____false

I work to help other family members ____true _____false

I feel I'm missing something important if
I don't focus on work all the time ____true _____false

It's just the money, that's why I do it ____true _____false

It's not easy to earn money-some are driven, some just do what is needed. We work hard every day to pay the bills, have a roof over our head and then we shop!

2-On our weekly trip to the grocery store, we know what we have to get, some dread it and some like it so much they go more than once a week. So let's ask

How many times a week do you pick up groceries: _____/week

Do you like being in the grocery store: _____ yes _____no

Do you do the shopping with someone else: ____ yes ____no

Who is your favorite person to take with you: _____

If you have kids, do you take them along: _____yes _____no

Are they helpful: _____yes _____no

Now we've all seen people in stores with children just wailing, crying and throwing tantrums. Yep, it happens everywhere I think. So if you have children, these are your questions

Have your children ever thrown a tantrum in the store _____yes _____no

Did you leave the store _____yes _____ no

Did you just let them cry it off _____yes _____ no

Well we can't help what happens sometimes. Kids will be kids.

3-Ever see those magazines by the check out? They're filled with the gossip of the famous. Those people get dragged through the mud, don't they? How you feel about those?

Do you read them _____yes _____ no

Do you buy the magazine _____yes _____ no

Do you believe them _____yes _____ no

What are your favorites to read: _____

_____

_____

4-Now with those types of articles you have to ask yourself some questions about the stars and far out tales. Just how important is it to your world?

Do you enjoy following celebrity lives _____yes _____ no

Do you agree with their lives being front-page _____yes _____ no

Is that the price of stardom _____yes _____ no

5-Now I'm presuming we all agree that at times those articles just go too far. Today I saw one showing an ex supermodel who had put on weight and they posted a front page of a pudgy stomach. Does that really matter in the grand scheme of my world? Nope…don't really care.

Even if aliens abducted her and she'd eaten too much and split the seams as they carried her away…as long as I get my groceries-I'm good!

In your opinion, what topics are really important to you about the famous? Number the following from 1-13 of the things you really think matter and everyone should know about celebs-(1 being most important)

Amount of money they make	_____	How they keep fit	_____
If they put on weight	_____	Who they're dating/married	_____
Where they travel	_____	Who they fight with	_____
If they're in rehab	_____	Where they live	_____
If they get arrested	_____	What they eat	_____
Who their kids are	_____	Where they shop	_____
How they cope with life	_____	What they're wearing	_____

Well I don't know, we all have opinions…but to me, they're just people who do something wonderful for a living and get paid well.

So if you could interview your favorite all time Star from one of those magazines and ask all the hard questions…

Who would that be? _____
Why?
_____

_____

_____

Which star do you think gets picked on the most? _____

I'm thinking the stars should publish their own magazine with responses to each tale of gossip. Just my opinion, but it would make it interesting to see them counter each comment the following month. Magazine wars!

6-There are so many things that we watch on TV or read in magazines that you gotta ask yourself…do we really believe it all? I'm not so sure. For me, I hate those commercials with young models telling me about anti age creams. You just shake your head...what are they thinking? Wouldn't it make more sense to use middle ages construction workers, fire fighters or police people…you know the type who really face stress, the elements and have no choice about harsh weather?

The commercials you hate most are for which product: _____

I guess I'm not in tune with the advertising world, because there is an abundance of commercials that just don't add up in my head. I'm going to list a few types of commercials, (let's pretend we're in advertising)-I'd like you to suggest a better commercial for each of the following.

For example:
I hate the diaper commercials when they have babies acting like they can talk. I never had children, so maybe moms relate to that one more. For me, it would be a way better commercial, watching a man go to change his baby and when he opens the diaper, he gags, reaches for clothespins and barbeque tongs, he just was surprised by what he found! Yep, I'd buy those diapers!

Let's start you with the one I just gave an example for:

A-Cutesy baby diaper commercials:

You'd like to see:

_____

_____

_____

_____

B-Women's foundation commercials-Those 14 year old girls with perfect skin to start with showing us how to cover up all our flaws. Don't know about you, but shouldn't they show flaws beforehand? Never seen an acne covered model saying, look…my skin is perfect now!

You'd like to see:

_____

_____

_____

_____

C-Now commercials for the allergy blockers, where people suddenly are standing in a bunch of leaves or in a field of flowers (like that happens every day)…If you had allergies would you tempt fate by going into the worst possible scenario?

You'd like to see:

_____

_____

_____

_____

D-Men's cologne commercials- I don't know about you, but I've given cologne to men I know and no magic happens afterwards (darn it)

You'd like to see:

_____

_____

_____

_____

E-Women's feminine protection commercials-Now really, do we ever wear bikini's and go on a yacht acting like we're happy as sunshine? Don't know about you, but I never have-(kinda moody actually). And do the men really show attraction and desire, thinking it's that happy time for us?

You'd like to see:

_____

_____

_____

_____

F-Male performance commercials-now some are cute and funny, like when you see the man skipping off to work or chores that get forgotten just to have that fulfilling afternoon. Yet you gotta wonder if you could come up with a better one, I know I could. (would they televise them?) You'd like to see:

_____

_____

_____

_____

We'll come back to more of these here and there…it's just too much fun being creative, isn't it?

7-Everyday we're inundated with ads, big sells, etc…seems they're everywhere in life. It's almost too much. You buy a magazine and have to skip 10 pages to continue the article you were reading to start with. Name the products that you see in magazines/newspapers.

What advertising do you to like seeing the most? _____

What advertising seems to be overdone? _____

Do you pay attention to the ads? _____yes _____no _____sometimes

Looking at yourself what product would you be best in a commercial for:

_____

Your friends would say:

_____

(Gotta love those friends, huh)

8-Ever see those commercials about treating yourself to a spa day? Man, I wish! My spa is a bubble bath at home and if I remember, I'll throw in a candle for ambience. Ok so I don't really pamper myself. If you could get one thing at a spa right now-

You would love to get: _____

9-A lot of commercials are about our well-being, getting a good night sleep or relaxing a bit more in life. I wonder how you relax on a regular basis. They say that's important since we have work, home, kids and schedules. It's a lot to fit into a day, isn't it?

So when you get home after your busy day and finally have time, how do you?

Normally unwind: _____

Do you make sure to put aside time just for you _____yes _____no

How often do you enjoy a hot/soothing bath _____times per week/month

Do you own a Jacuzzi/spa tub _____yes _____ no

Do you wish for one regularly _____yes _____ no

Do you work out to get some of the stress out _____yes _____ no

If you have family, do you take time to catch up _____yes _____ no

What time of the night do you normally begin to feel relaxed? I guess if you work the night shift it could be in the morning: _____am/pm

10- Some people never feel really relaxed, do they? If you own a hamster like mine, it goes twenty four-seven. Always thinking of things to be done or want to do, the schedules and plans. Yep, at times it goes and goes. How often do you feel totally rested when you get up in the morning?

Out of 7 days of the week, I feel totally rested only _____ days.

11- Today everything seems so fast and we are in such a hurry to do stuff. Whether it's our tight schedules or things we try to fit into every day. I'm sure if you have kids, you have crazy schedules, but for some singles, it's the social life, gym, home and friends. We're all in such a hurry and looking around a grocery store it shows, doesn't it? The world of pre-packaged, ready to go meals…don't know if they're good for us, but I'm eating one right now. TV dinners at times are the quick way to get through. So let's see how you do in this department:

Do you buy any of the following ready frozen/ packaged food

TV Dinners (traditional type)	_____yes	_____no
Frozen Pizza	_____yes	_____no
Frozen Pizza Pops/Burritos etc.…	_____yes	_____no
Frozen pasta dishes-heat n serve	_____yes	_____no
Ready-made chicken/roasts etc.…	_____yes	_____no
Ready-made salads/coleslaws	_____yes	_____no
Ready-made desserts	_____yes	_____no

12- Well if you do buy some of those, let's ask a few more questions. Now these are from your grocery store…not take-out or the drive-through.

I eat pre-packaged meals at home _____ times a week

I serve my family pre-packaged meals _____times a week

I have served dinner guests pre-packaged meals ____frequently ____never _____on occasion

13-Yep, they make it easy for us to keep on the move. Most of the time I cook, yet there are those times I'm just too busy. There are certain meals you plan for, like the traditional holiday meals-I love making those! My favorite is Thanksgiving...I've done a couple with the big turkey and all the trimmings.

What is or would be your favorite holiday meal to cook:

_____

If you could arrange to do the next one and you got to make whatever you wanted, your menu would be: (top 10 items)

_____   _____

_____   _____

_____   _____

_____   _____

_____   _____

Now it's a big production doing a meal that size and I've had my moments and tough spots. The one thing I hate most about cooking that turkey is taking the stuff out of it...the gizzards (EWW!) That is a gag-me moment for about 2 minutes of dry heaving and nausea. Do you have any EWW moments?

You don't like to:

_____

A friend once left that bag inside and cooked it along with the bird, by accident-ICK! How about sharing something you or someone you know did whilst cooking that meal. Something that just was oh so wrong, but funny!

Who was it _____

What did they do:

_____

_____

14- Well let's jump back to the commercial side of life. It's time to think about all the time we spend at the grocery store. It's part of life-shopping for food. Some love it and for some of us-it's a pain! Let's see where you stand on it all. What best describes your grocery store habits:

Get what ya need and get out	_____	Go up and down every aisle	_____
Follow the list you have	_____	Divide and conquer (give half the list to your partner/children)	_____
The browser-look at everything	_____	Escape artist-send someone else	_____
Online-order groceries	_____	Buy only what you have coupons for	_____

15- Grocery stores have so many wonderful things. They even have those sample people offering you food. I often think if I stop right after work at a few stores I won't need to make dinner when I get home. If I did that five days a week I could reduce my grocery costs immensely.

Do you usually sample stuff _____ yes _____ no

How often have you been so impressed you bought the product right away: _____ %

Do you go back for more _____ yes _____ no

Does your partner linger there while you continue shopping _____ yes _____ no

What things don't you ever trust sampling _____

16- When shopping, we all have a pattern, we'll start in one place usually and follow the same pattern from one end of the store to the other, especially on those big shopping days. We visit the same store and know where everything is already. The following is a list of departments found in every grocery store, mark these in the order you visit first to last: 1-18.

Deli	_____	Bakery	_____
Produce	_____	Pharmacy (if one)	_____
Cleaning aisle	_____	Snack aisle	_____

Frozen foods	_____	Meats	_____
Floral	_____	Tin goods	_____
Soft drink/water aisle	_____	Dairy	_____
Cheese	_____	Fish	_____
Paper-toilet/Kleenex	_____	Pet supplies	_____
Coffee/Spices	_____	Toothpaste/mouthwash	_____

17-Shopping takes up quite a bit of time in our lives. Everything we need, we have to go buy. Now if you need something for home repairs you go to a different store and home décor is a different one too. So, let's see your favorite places to shop for each of these: Name your favorites stores:

Groceries	_____	Clothing	_____
Home repair	_____	Furniture	_____
Electronics	_____	Music	_____
Kid's toys	_____	Books	_____
Home décor	_____	Bakery items	_____
Greeting Cards	_____	Sporting goods	_____
Pharmacy	_____	Childs clothing	_____
Material (sewing/crafts)	_____	Christmas gifts	_____
Auto parts	_____	Paint	_____

I'm sure you have many more stores you visit, but these are the basics.

18-I like shopping kinda/sorta, but the perfect scenario would be if there wasn't anyone else in the store and I'd get what I need and get out. Yep I seem to lack in the patience department. I'm a polite shopper, but some things drive me nuts, what about you?

On a scale from 1-10, mark at what level things annoy you when in a store (1 being you'd just like to poke them in the eye and 10 being I don't mind)

People who leave carts in the middle of the aisle   _____

Things on the shelves that you can't reach   _____

No sales associates available to you   _____

That line up at the cashier   _____

People walking slowly not paying attention   _____

Groups of people standing in the way talking   _____

People who clip your heels with the cart   _____

Fussy people making a point while you're waiting   _____

Kids running around parents not watching them   _____

Those announcements you don't quite hear   _____

Cashiers busy gossiping with each other   _____

Messy shelves when you can't find anything   _____

Prices not clearly marked (anywhere)   _____

When the registers don't bring up the sale price   _____

If I missed it, what one thing do you dislike the most

_____

19-This one is for the gentlemen out there. I am amazed at those shaving commercials. It started with double bladed razors then to three, now to four or five. How many blades do you need? Let's ask you men then:

What kind of razor do you use _____

Do you try the new ones on the market _____yes _____ no

Any difference with number of blades really _____yes _____no

You have tried how many kinds of razors so far _____

How many blades do you figure they'll stop at _____

Now the commercials always show Mr. Young Rugged (in his mid20's I'm sure) and he has a woman come up at the end and rub his face. Now I'm betting that doesn't happen every morning in your house, does it? Just as I've never seen the commercial with little wads of toilet paper all over the place.

So gents, what would sell you on a new razor? You'd like to see a commercial:

_____

_____

Now ladies, we use them too and I have never felt like a 20 year old goddess afterwards. Maybe I'm not using the right one, but usually there is a bit of swearing going on whilst I try to stop the bleeding ankle for the next 2 hours.

So ladies, what do you think would be a better commercial for the girly razor? You'd like to see:

_____

_____

20-You're giggling now aren't ya? Ah, the world of advertising! It drives what we buy and things we didn't even know we needed. For me, I get curious about all those vitamins to be healthier. Yep, I do take the time to research them after I see a commercial. I don't buy them all, but I do check things out. So is there any one type of commercial that sparks you to look into something more thoroughly?
I usually check out or research (when I see a new commercial)

_____

21-In the grocery store world, we all have our own way of picking the produce…don't fib, you do it to and we watch other people choose their produce. So what are your methods? Check off what you normally do.

____I am a thumper   ____I squeeze   ____I sniff

____I pick through it all   ____I weigh it   ____I balance one in each hand

____I ask for help

The curious things we see in a grocery store and it's not limited to produce aisle's either. Ever notice those people who read labels on everything? It's the trend to make sure you know what's in it all.

Do you check labels ____yes ____no

What are the ingredients you check for the most?

_____   _____   _____   _____

With this new be healthy motto lifestyle, we all try to be a little more conscious of what we buy, so are you fussy about your veggies?

You buy from the grocery store produce section   ____yes ____no

You buy from the organically grown section   ____yes ____no

You buy direct from farmer's markets or growers   ____yes ____no

You grow your own   ____yes ____no

You order from organic distributors   ____yes ____no

22-Well with all the food options these days, it's getting confusing what to buy. I mean they have whole wheat's, multi grains, BL probiotics, omega rich, anti-oxidants-so many different things…

So on average you buy the healthy choice _____% of the time

You stick to your favorites _____% of the time

How often do you try something healthy _____ times per month

In the past 5 years, you find you eat more of which health foods: top 3 please

_____ _____ _____

With all the fiber health hype lately, switching cold turkey would probably put my body into shock…I'd be on the toilet for days I'm sure. Have you eased into it or dove right in?

I have _____

It still confounds me the amount of additives they put in our food. I would prefer if they stopped using all that stuff, got rid of pesticides and hormone fed animals. Funny the people that don't use chemicals or additives charge even more for their product...why is that? If they don't have to pay for chemicals…shouldn't it be cheaper?

23- They say we don't get enough vitamins from our food intake anymore. The saying is 7-10 servings of vegetables/fruit per day to keep optimum health. And yet, studies constantly bring up we are deficient in one thing or another. Now what would you say about yourself:

You eat properly at least _____ days in a week

You only eat take out about _____times per month

Do you take vitamins/supplements daily _____yes _____no

What supplements do you take regularly-name some of them:

_____ _____ _____ _____

_____ _____ _____ _____

_____ _____ _____ _____

24-There are drinks now to boost our intake, a convenient drink to swallow what you need. Funny, the old saying was to be sure to take vitamins in between bites of food so they get absorbed...now you can just drink them.

Have you tried one of these new drinks _____yes _____ no

If you have, do you find a difference _____yes _____ no

Health conscious is a good thing and we all try to follow along. Some even create their own protein shakes or fruit smoothies. We've all tried those and some have found what works for them.
Are you a home smoothie person _____yes _____no

If yes, what is your recipe: _____ _____

_____ _____ _____

_____

How often to you drink this blended stuff _____ times per day

25-Let's take a break from the health stuff. There are so many things advertised that we all try or would like to. We see them on TV or on the shopping channels-gadgets, processors, etc...

Name one thing you'd like to try, right this very second if the manufacturer gave it to you for free

_____

26-They say that 2/3rds of the population is overweight. Some it's just a smidge, while others have a few more, yet in advertising, it seems most of the time the products are shown by tiny size 0-3 people. That confounds me a bit. If the majority of people are bigger, why are commercials from the thin? Yep one of those things you just wonder about. If the majority of the consumers are overweight, wouldn't it be smarter to use real people? We'd all like a model's income, wouldn't we?

I have made a list of products you see advertised all the time. Mark beside each, what body type you've most often seen advertisers use to sell the product and in the second column, mark what you think would be more effective.

T=thin, A=average, P = a few pounds, E=extra baggage. N=makes no difference

Sporting event   _____   _____

Make up   _____   _____

Cologne   _____   _____

Cooking gadget   _____   _____

Travel   _____   _____

Fine dining   _____   _____

Fast food   _____   _____

Jewelry   _____   _____

Retail clothing   _____   _____

Perfume   _____   _____

Weight loss product   _____   _____

Electronics   _____   _____

Household cleaners   _____   _____

The world of advertising is designed to get us to think from new and different angles. I guess it's working, although I wonder what would happen if they had more everyday people in them with real situations? Like when you see commercials for plumbers, it's always a well-dressed man, they never show the one that bends under the sink and you see way more than you ever wanted to.

27-We all have daily things we have to deal with. We've covered the grocery store, now what about all the other things we end up needing? You hear the commercials or watch them, so let's see who stands out in your mind for each of these. Think fast though, first name that comes to mind. Who would you call based on the ads for each of the following?

When the car breaks down you go to:_____

Need a new muffler you'd take it to: _____

Got pests, you'd call: _____

Been in an accident call: _____

House insurance from: _____

Car insurance from: _____

Need a new mattress go to: _____

Those are just a few to start with, we'll keep asking throughout the book. I bet you didn't have to think long about these, you probably repeated the ad in your head and got that song stuck in there now.

28- I bet you have a few commercials that just stand out in your head as the dumbest or most annoying of all. Doesn't matter if it was recent or from way back when. I know I still remember the "don't hate me because I'm beautiful" line. I hated her just because she repeatedly told me not to!

What was the worst line you can remember, from a commercial that you still roll your eyes at:

_____

List three more lines from commercials that just sucked in your opinion:

_____

_____

_____

29- Along with those are the best commercial characters! Here, we have a Bison that does the commercials for the phone company. Yep, he stands out in my mind. Those lovable characters who become synonymous with the product.

Who is the most memorable character for you to date?

_____

Commercial was for what product/place

_____

Now with that, there have been people or animals that stood the test of time. Let's see if you can name a few that have somehow become synonymous with the products they sold. Off the top of your head, what is the first character that pops into your head for each? (if you can't remember the actual name just describe the character)

Cat food: _____

Coffee: _____

Fast food restaurant: _____

Toilet paper: _____

Floor cleaner: _____

Mexican food: _____

Beer: _____

Salad dressing: _____

Tuna: _____

We just remember them automatically, don't we?

30-Now holiday commercials are wonderful. My favorite all time commercial was for a soft drink company that had the big semi-truck driving through mountains all lit up and the town would light up as it drove through. That stands out for me.

What is your favorite holiday commercial

What was the product:_____

Describe the commercial

_____

_____

31-Now catch phrases are a part of any commercial and we automatically think of the product when you hear it. Let's see if you remember who these catch phrases belong to:

1-zoom, zoom, zoom   _____

2-I'd like to teach the world to sing   _____

3-Put a tiger in your tank   _____

4-plop plop, fizz fizz   _____

5-heartburn, naseau, upset stomach…   _____

6-finger licking good   _____

7-RRRRR Billy-Hello Captain   _____

8-Nothin says lovin like   _____

9-Two all beef patties, special sauce, lettuce, cheese, pickles, onions on a sesame seed bun
                                                 _____

10-Mmm mmm good   _____

11-A little dab will do ya   _____

12-don't leave home without it   _____

32-Think back to your early childhood with all those commercials that planted ideas in your head for birthdays and Christmas: I was around 4 and remember bugging my parents for a doll for my birthday. Surrounded by childhood friends, I unwrapped one with blonde short hair that came with its own lil plastic tub, I was so excited! It wasn't the one I had seen, but mom and dad knew it was my hearts wish and they struggled financially to buy it. They watched as I undressed it that first time to give it a bath then were horrified to find out my little boy doll was anatomically correct. Yep, they didn't expect to see that and worried at the other children's reactions. It is the first gift I remember wanting and will never forget it.

What was the first commercial you remember seeing as a child and wishing for as a gift?

It was a _____

Did you get it _____ yes _____ no

If yes, describe in three words that first moment:

_____   _____   _____

What was the most exciting Christmas gift you ever got?

_____

33- From the time we're young until the time we pass, they advertise so many things. I remember being excited by many things. My folks did manage to get us a few of those real special things over the years. Name the four best toys you saw advertised and wanted when you were a child:

_____   _____

_____   _____

34- One Christmas when I was 5 or so, my parents really outdid themselves. They spent a few months before Christmas downstairs every night in the basement and there was constant noise. My older sister and I were told we couldn't go downstairs and they'd lock up every night after they came up. We were always trying to find a way to go downstairs, but never did. Well Christmas morning we got our very first official "Barbie and Pepper" dolls. That was really something since we didn't have a lot of money.

The next present we each opened was a hand-made closet, complete with drawers and tiny little rods to hang clothes. And inside, were all these handmade Barbie clothes, from ball gowns to swim wear. We understood the months downstairs, the work and time put into that is something we only really figured out later. What some people will do to please others is amazing! There must have been 50 outfits for each doll.

Did you ever receive a special gift? What was it and from who? Share your special memory:

_____

_____

_____

_____

_____

35- I'm sure everywhere we look and everything we do has been something we've seen in some form of advertising. From where we eat, what we eat, where we go, to what we drive…yep, it makes the world go round! Off the top of your head, who has the most memorable ad campaigns in your opinion for each of these (Name the company)

Fast food chain _____

Cruise line _____

Airline _____

Hotel chain _____

Restaurant _____

Sports complex _____

Toy store _____

Department store _____

Car manufacturer _____

36- Lets have some fun with more catch phrases. How many can you remember this time?

1- You deserve a break today _____

2- Let your fingers do the walking _____

3-Keeps going and going and going _____

4-Melts in your mouth not on your hands _____

5-I love you, you love me _____

6-Can you hear me now? _____

7-Good to the last drop _____

8-They're great _____

9-Have it your way _____

10-You're in good hands _____

37-Let's play advertiser again –Like in question (6) sometimes we'd have better ideas for things we'd like to see.

A-All those make up commercials, I tell ya they make you believe you could really look like those models if you buy the product. Those girls are usually young and born beautiful. I say use people who aren't born stunning and make them look fantastic-I may just buy it then. What famous people do you think would be more convincing if you could see the before and after.

You'd like them to show before and after make-up shots of (top 6)

_____   _____

_____   _____

_____   _____

B-Those live talk chat lines, I mean really, do they honestly think we believe its Ms. or Mr. Perfect is sitting on the other end? (I'm not buying it!) They always show those sexy people sitting at home on the phone-yeah right! Who you believe is on the other end of the line?

Describe what you envision:

_____

C-Those upset stomach/diarrhea commercials...you know the one where they do a cute little dance? In real life there is nothing cute or funny when that dance happens-(well only if it happens to someone else maybe.) To me they should show a high-speed chase where that person in the car stops for nothing...you've been there, haven't ya?

You would advertise this by:

_____

_____

_____

D-Another one I just don't get is the heartburn commercials. It shows someone at a diner eating a whole pile of greasy food. Well you gotta shake your head at that. If you get indigestion or heartburn...don't you usually avoid eating that kind of stuff?

A better commercial for heartburn/indigestion would be:

_____

_____

_____

38-There are many commercials now for medicinal products. You've heard them...the ones saying if you experience this or that, ask your doctor about-whatever the drug name. Is it me or does there seem to be too many drugs available on the market? And how come the doctors don't know about them? You diagnose yourself and you have to tell them? The side effects....yikes!

I often think about the trade-off. How bad do you have to feel before you risk the side-effects...know what I mean? If you have sleeping problems are you really willing to risk drowsiness and vomiting the whole next day? Or if you have a headache, is it worth having diarrhea and upset stomach but no headache?

Have you ever used one of these and ended up trading off ____yes ____no

Did it solve the original problem ____yes ____no

What was the trade-off:

No more _____ but got _____

No more _____ but got _____

Did you tell your doctor about the new type of medicine available _____ yes _____ no

I wonder how many try these things without consulting a doctor first. Rather scary to think what could happen with mixing medications.

39-Advertising that I totally don't understand is the 'find out your credit score.' Don't know about you, but I usually know what my credit rating is by the bank's response of NO!

So gotta ask:

Do you know your credit score	_____ yes	_____ no
Does it give you peace of mind	_____ yes	_____ no
Did the answer surprise you	_____ yes	_____ no
Did you know previously where you stood financially	_____ yes	_____ no
Did knowing it change your habits	_____ yes	_____ no
Have you ever been able to convince the banker to give you the money based on knowing your score	_____ yes	_____ no
Who do you give your score to	_____ yes	_____ no
How much bartering power does that give you	_____ %	

40-Money, money, money, it makes the world go round. If we're not making it, we're spending it. So let's find out about your spending habits. I would define myself as a

Budget person-I plan for it all _____yes _____no

A bargain shopper-if it's not on sale I don't get it _____yes _____no

A comparison shopper-shop around for best price _____yes _____no

Impulse buyer-I see it, I get it _____yes _____no

Whim shopper-I buy what I want-not need _____yes _____no

Frugal-I tend to watch what I buy closely _____yes _____no

What is your weakness? We all have that one thing that when we see it on sale, we just buy it: (For me it's music CD's)

_____

41-With shopping, there are things we want and things we need. I'm going to presume you buy all the basic needs like food, gitch, clothing etc…the everyday stuff. But at times there are things we've put off getting either due to cost or lack of funds. We have to do without it or have to plan for it as a future purchase if it's something we really want.

Right now, I need to buy a _____

I managed to get _____% of the monthly things I needed

I am saving any extra cash because I'd need to replace or repair:

_____

If I had an extra $500.00 right now I would probably spend it on:

_____

Now, if we have a partner in life, at times they spend money where we may not feel it should be spent. What may seem necessary to one may not seem necessary to the other. And if you asked them, I'm sure they'd think you spend too much on something as well. It's about individual choice really. So you think

Your partner spends too much money on: _____

You think you spend too much money on: _____

Your partner thinks you spend too much money on: _____

I know this is a delicate subject for couples, but it's just how it is. We really spend a lot of energy discussing different ideals at times.

42-So how are you with money? Me, I'm ok until I get those surprise repairs. I manage to somehow find a way to fix things or do without. In this day and age, it's hard to make ends meet…let alone the little extra's we all need. With the cost of goods, it's just crazy at times to make it all work. So looking at your overall money handling, you would say you're:

A paycheck-to-paycheck person Bills are paid, food on the table!	_____yes	_____no
You are able to put away a little here n there	_____yes	_____no
You are comfortable	_____yes	_____no
You are smart with it and doing just fine	_____yes	_____no
A breeze, you live life pretty well	_____yes	_____no
A Whiz, you have the good life all the way around	_____yes	_____no
Struggling-you pay what you can, when you can	_____yes	_____no
Overwhelmed, you need debt solutions and fast	_____yes	_____no

43-It's not easy. Nope, we work hard every day and we want to be comfortable. For some people it's the biggest worry in everyday life, while others don't fret over it all. In general you worry about your financial picture:

You worry about finances _____% of the time.

Your biggest concern seems to always be:

_____

If you could make one monthly payment disappear, you'd like to pay off your

_____

44-Well it all takes time I suppose. There are those who work two jobs all the time just to make ends meet. Some do that just to enjoy the little extras in life.

When is the last time you went on a vacation _____

What was your last big purchase   _____

What big items do you hope to or need to purchase in the next 5 years? If you own a house for example, at times you know you'll need a new washer or stove soon. Or maybe it's a family get a way. So realistically you hope to purchase:

_____   _____   _____

_____   _____   _____

45-If you own a house you know that there is always something that needs to be done. And when you got the fixes all done, you at times decide to decorate, renovate or improve.

When is the last time you decorated your home _____

When is the last time you had to repair something _____

If you had extra money right now you'd probably

Begin a new project   _____yes _____no

Finish some old ones _____ yes _____ no

Renovate _____ yes _____ no Which room: _____

Do yard Reno's _____ yes _____ no

Do some updating _____ yes _____ no

Re-decorate _____ yes _____ no

46-They have TV shows that just show us how to do it, don't they? Design shows, repair shows, the how to series. Do you watch them?

Your favorite home design show to watch _____

Your favorite renovation show to watch _____

Your super hero for repairs would be _____

If you could have any one from any of those shows come and re-do the décor in your home, you would:

Definitely get: _____

47-Are you ready to try a few more catch phrases?

1-For all you do this   _____

2-Oh thank heaven for   _____

3-You're soaking in it!   _____

4-Do you eat the red one's last   _____

5-The San Francisco treat   _____

6-My baloney has a first name   _____

7-I'm a pepper, he's a pepper   _____

8-Maybe she's born with it, maybe _____

9-Snap-crackle-pop _____

10-Good to the last drop _____

48-Seems things have changed for kids nowadays. I remember the days of old when you were lucky to get a present and you'd be thankful, no matter what it was. Seems today the kids want the best or most popular everything. For some, if they don't get it…yikes! They even steal it from one another. Sad what kids sometimes do now.

Do you buy for kids, (your own or others) _____yes _____ no

Do you find they want specific things _____yes _____ no

Do you always buy the name brands they ask for _____yes _____ no

What would happen if you didn't? _____

Would they still thank you for the gift _____yes _____ no

Would they be upset if it wasn't exact _____yes _____ no

49-The commercial world even applies to clothing for kids. This past while I've heard parents talking of buying clothes from a designer for their children-seems it's all about the name. Half of the designers I've even heard of…I'm outta the loop on this one.

So let's see if you're in the loop-Name the top 5 brands of clothing kids want today:

_____ _____

_____ _____

_____

Does it last any longer than generic _____yes _____no

Does it look all that different than generic _____yes _____no

Do you find it makes them take care of it more _____yes _____no

50-I have nephews and when I can, I try to get things they want although I can't always afford it. I don't notice much of a difference…a jacket is a jacket -two arms, a front and a back and if it keeps you warm it does the job. Even the games today are targeted at specifics. It used to be any game would do, but now they want the brands. They outgrow it fast enough and you end up giving it away or putting it in a garage sale.

So when you look at all the toys or gifts you've bought for children in your life:

You would say you pay _____% higher price just for the name

How often do you buy the top brand they want _____% of time

How often do you see them take care of it more than the generic _____% of the time

How much excess money would you guess you've invested into the name brand over the past year: $_____

51-It's amazing when you walk through the toy aisles in a store-the stuff they have is incredible! We had building blocks, they have entire packages where you can build cities or space-crafts and it goes on, and on…. It's all in the hype and packaging. Why don't they just make generic different shaped blocks and that way kids could build whatever they want if they are imaginative enough…oh that's right…it's branding.

Looking back from when you were young, how do you think kids today compare?

You would say kids use their own imagination _____% of the time

You would say kids keep themselves busy _____% of the time

You would say kids watch TV _____% more than you ever did

You would say their creativity level is _____% of what yours was as a child.

You would say kids play video/computer games _____% of the time

You would like to see kids do more
1_____

2_____

3_____

52-Now video/computer games are not just a child's world anymore. They have some that are pretty realistic-almost like watching a movie for me. I've watched friends play and I'm astounded at what graphics can do, not like back when video's first started. Did you have any favorites way back then

Your favorite pinball machine was _____

Your favorite arcade game was _____

You always got top score on _____

The easiest game for you back then was _____

The one you never conquered was _____

Do you play video games now _____ yes _____ no

Your favorite so far would be _____

Do you play against others through the Internet _____ yes _____ no

How many hours do you play per week _____

53-Along came fitness tapes and dvds…think over the years at how many fitness programs or equipment they've come out with. I've tried a few along the way-tapes for working out and the stationary bikes, stair climbers -(great place to hang clothes to dry)

Did you buy fitness programs _____ yes _____ no

What about fitness equipment _____ yes _____ no

How many different programs have you bought _____

Which one did you keep up the longest with _____

How many pieces of equipment have you bought _____

The one that worked the best for you was_____

How long did you keep it up _____ days/weeks/months/years

54-So many things that are designed to help us get fit. Even the Stars promote their own programs/equipment. Those late night infomercials you just happen to catch the new and exciting-etc…

Which Star's equipment do you recall seeing the most
_____

You always wanted to try which celebrity's equipment?
_____

I wonder why they chose celebrities-I always picture their life as having personal trainers, professional cooks…why would they pitch a product? Wouldn't it be more believable to have them use everyday people using the products?

55-Many celebrities put out their own plans for working out on the market. Think back to all the one's you've tried and in your opinion-

Who is the best motivator _____

Who had the best routine to follow _____

You absolutely have gotten into what activity by starting with one of these programs

_____

Enough fitness for now!

56-Now every week-(sometimes twice a week) you get flyers in the mail. Heck probably in some places you get them every day! Now I take them all to a friend who loves to browse these things. I do page through quickly and then they're forgotten.

How many flyers would you say you get in a week _____

Out of the bunch, how many do you page through _____

Do you start a list of what and where to go   _____yes _____ no

Do you follow the list   _____yes _____ no

57-I know some stores may have some stuff cheaper and then others have different products on sale. It's a lot of maneuvering around to catch each sale. You'd have to be a planner for that.

How far do you usually have to travel for the sale items _____ miles

Do you find you hop from one store to the next a lot _____ yes _____ no

If you had to calculate the gas you spend traveling to each, do you think it's still worth the trip, and running around for the following

Grocery items	_____ yes	_____ no	Clothing	_____ yes	_____ no
Household goods	_____ yes	_____ no	Furniture	_____ yes	_____ no
Electronics	_____ yes	_____ no	Building products	_____ yes	_____ no

Do you sometimes wish they'd just stop sending flyers _____ yes _____ no

Do you feel it would be better to have a mass online flyer of your weekly deals then you could save all the paper and just see online where, when, how much _____ yes _____ no

58-There sure is a lot of reality shows on TV now, from the housewife life to finding your partner, even racing across the world. So many things that people will just go through for a chance at money or fame. Don't know if you watch any of them but if you had to, which three would you participate in?

#1_____ #2_____

  #3_____

The good thing about these shows, people just like you and me could perhaps get our 15 minutes of fame. Although I don't if I'd like being followed around 24-7 with a camera, but I guess it's a way of life for some. Some of the shows just seem downright strange to be promoting. There are several I just shake my head at, so how do you feel

On a scale from 1-10 (1 being love the idea-10 disagree with it)

Mulitple birth families   _____

Large familys   _____

Small people   _____

Family swaps-trading spouse's   _____

Filthy house's   _____

Dancing competitions   _____

Talent competitions   _____

Surgical adjustments   _____

Finding a partner   _____

Strangers sharing a house   _____

Surviving   _____

Kid's beauty   _____

Cooking or baking   _____

The rich people's everyday lives   _____

So many different types of shows spotlighting the everyday people and the crazy things they can do or will do. Some are downright funny and some-no comment.

59-Notice now how everyone has a card you need to carry? Yep, my wallet gets bigger and bigger and it's not due to money, but all those buying club cards. How's your wallet?

How many buying cards would you say you have in total   _____

How many air mile collecting cards do you have   _____

Do you have any prepaid cards for shopping-how many   _____

Do you remember to always use your cards   _____

Now since you already wrote down how many club cards do you have-go count them.

Total club cards in my wallet right now: _____

60-Seems everyone has their own card and to get one you have to fill out a detailed form where you share all your info. Even with cash purchases they ask you a whole bunch of personal questions. Do they really need to know where I live if I've paid cash? It really annoys me.

How many times have you:

Had to give out your info for a simple cash transaction   _____

Do you always comply   _____ yes _____ no

Do you think they should have this info   _____ yes _____ no

How many companies now know everything about you do you think _____

61-The TV world brings so many options to our life-new ideals, outlooks and they now have many shows fixing up us everyday people. Seems we don't all put our best foot forward every day. Fashion, hairstyle, cosmetics, surgical alteration, dental-repair-the possibilities are endless!

Do you like these make over shows   _____ yes _____ no

Would you like to be on one   _____ yes _____ no

You believe your style is (check one)

A perfect fit for who you are   _____

Could use some tweaking   _____

Need of an overhaul   _____

Hopeless   _____

So, if you could be on one of these shows and get that whole make over, you would like to be a guest on:

_____

62-Now with going on one of these shows you're asked to totally give yourself up to their expert care. They have professionals in every aspect of the make-over. What do you think would be the hardest thing for you to adjust to or go through? Put these in order of what you'd look forward to going through the most.(#1-being I can't wait for that first and so on.)

Clothing   _____

Hairstyle   _____

Attitude about your appearance   _____

Minor Surgical procedures
(vision correction, botox injections etc…)   _____

Dental work   _____

Old habits   _____

Viewing yourself with a new outlook   _____

Positive thinking   _____

Learning to take time for yourself   _____

Applying cosmetics daily   _____

Accepting your body   _____

63-Well with looking at the self-image on TV today…they now have many shows spotlighting the wealthy and how they live. The spending, inter-relationship turmoil and problems they experience. I suppose it allows us to glimpse how the other half lives and how they cope with their world. Some can relate and for others, they just don't see the importance in watching.

Do you enjoy watching the wealthy in daily life   yes_____ no _____

Do you feel a sense of connection with them   yes_____ no _____

What three things most shock you about their way of life

_____

_____

_____

64-Some of these people work and some don't. It seems their lives are very different from what I know and I wonder if you feel the same. If you could sit down with these wealthy people and have a heart to heart conversation with a couple of them, what would be your 5 top questions for them?

1-_____

2-_____

3-_____

4-_____

5-_____

65-So many shows about different people today-Wedding planners, bakers, children competing for crowns, cars being tricked out, fitness…it's amazing the worlds we get to see. We get to watch so many different facets of life and things we never even knew existed. What's your opinion on this all?

Name 5 reality shows that you've seen and think they are absolutely wonderful and have brought something special into your life

1-_____

2-_____

3-_____

4-_____

5-_____

Now name 5 reality shows that you think are a total waste of time. Whether you've glimpsed them momentarily or actually sat through a few episodes:

1-_____

2-_____

3-_____

4-_____

5-_____

66-Times have changed, haven't they? Things we used to never think of advertising are plastered everywhere in life. From hardship to success- inspirational to unbelievable!

Just as with food advertising, seems it used to be quick solutions for meals was what they sold us-now we're hearing more of going natural and organic-back to traditional thinking. It's hard to know what is best anymore, isn't it? You often hear of recalls, additives being toxic, long-term side-effects of various things they invented only recently to make our life easier. It really makes you stop and question....who is looking out for us really?

Think back the past several years...I'm sure you remember products that were supposed to be safe and wonderful, the new way of living. For example the diet solutions...these new found additives to reduce sugar intake. Yet now there are many questions about what it can or may do in the long run. But there are so many others that we hear of daily.

List 6 products that you have heard something recently as being questionable for your health:

_____   _____   _____

_____   _____   _____

67-Wait! Let's think on this all for a minute. I wonder how these all managed to get on the shelves at the store. Everything has to pass some sort of testing period, right? So why do we have dangerous things on the shelves? Who do you think should be responsible for making sure it is a safe product? Number these 1-4 in order of who should be liable.

Individual people who purchase it _____   The manufacturer _____

The advertisers who sell the idea _____   The government _____

68-Now with time it is becoming standard to list ingredients, yet unless you're a scientist…you can't really decipher which are more dangerous than others. Don't you wish they had a scale label on the product? Like a (1-10) box that would show the percentage of harmful toxic ingredients. (#1 would be completely safe and #10 would be use at your own risk) At least we'd stand a fighting chance at picking the safer products. Now of course some products just are harmful yet needed, paint thinners, ammonia, etc… What would you like to see to improve the situation (3 suggestions)

_____

_____

_____

69-Lets have some more fun with creating our own commercials. Like before, I will mention a product and how I've seen it advertised and you get to be creative in how you'd like to see it promoted:

A-Toilet tissue commercials-Now I don't know about you, but I've never likened the use of the paper to a puppy, kitten, or an angel…I guess you would want it to be as soft as one I suppose. And there is nothing angelic about the moment when you're using it really.

You'd like to see a commercial for toilet paper as:

_____

_____

_____

B-Birth control-So many to choose from. Some sing a happy song, even have one with synchronized swimming (don't quite get either of those), but that's just me. I'd much prefer seeing a lady out on a date with Mr. Perfect-she excuses herself and goes to the washroom to make sure that she did in fact take that pill this morning-big happy smile "Woo Hoo-it's all good!"
You'd like to see a birth control commercial:

_____

_____

_____

C-All those air fresheners on the market-mood settings, fragrance relief, aromatherapy-endless the amount of gadgets or containers. Some you just plug in and it's like the whole world changes around you. Some ads have cartoon animals using them to freshen the place, I've often wondered why is there no disgruntled mood one's? If I'm having a bad day shouldn't I have the option of throwing in the dark and grumpy scent?

You'd like to see an air freshener commercial which:

_____

_____

_____

70-Man those are fun! I think I'm aiming at a new career, what about you? We would take the world by storm with our ideas and commercials! Now we've poked fun at a few of the concepts and yet there are those that just stand out as great commercials. The one's we end up laughing, every time we see them or it brings tears to our eyes.

For me I love those counting sheep or the commercial for a new rice dish with less salt-that little saltshaker ends up on the fire escape and tears (salt) pours from those two little holes that are his eyes. Yep I think that is just too cute!

Your favorite would be for which product: _____

The commercial would be described as follows:

_____

_____

_____

The world of advertising just fascinates me. Could you imagine being in a boardroom just tossing fun, crazy ways to sell something? I'm thinking it would be a dream job!

71-With advertising comes the music side of things. The jingles, songs…whatever it takes to get the point across to appeal to buyers.

What is the most memorable song you've seen used in a commercial?

_____

What is the worst song ever used in a commercial?

_____

72-With thinking about those, I once saw a video of appropriate songs for the products. It was a comedian's way of poking fun at the industry. I think I laughed for 10 minutes after I saw that video. So let's ask you to pick from the songs you know, what would use in each of these:

Car commercial _____

Shampoo commercial _____

Condom commercial _____

Jewelry commercial _____

Sleep aide commercial _____

73-Now advertising isn't always on the Radio or TV, nope you get it for all kinds of services delivered right to your door. Some can be a one-page flyer and sometimes people come to talk to you about it all.

What was the last one page flyer you received for a service?

_____

What was the last person trying to talk to you about at your door?

_____

What was the last telemarketer that called trying to sell you?

_____

Seems there is nowhere safe to get away from people trying to sell an idea, product, or service. We even get those calls to survey us in order to figure out what we feel works and doesn't. What was the last survey you actually participated in on the phone?

_____

74-Funny how at a time of thinking green and reducing waste we get so much paper by way of advertising. Thinking on the saving the planet-we should ask, what you do in your home? Now each place is different in what they recycle so

In your area do they have a program to recycle all of the following?

Plastics	_____yes	_____no
Glass	_____yes	_____no
Styrofoam	_____yes	_____no
Tins	_____yes	_____no
Metal	_____yes	_____no
Paper	_____yes	_____no
Cardboard	_____yes	_____no

Now some places even have guidelines to dispose of certain products which are harmful. Batteries, paints, chemicals…

Does your area have such a program? _____ yes _____ no

Do you always follow the guidelines? _____ yes _____ no

75-So let's see how you do with it all. There are those who diligently follow the program and those who don't. I'm sure we do our best, but some just find the nearest dumpster and toss it.

Could be your cleaning out the car or straightening out the garage and it's just easier than sorting into the proper bins.

You recycle each from the above list what percentage of the time?

Plastics	_____%	Glass	_____%
Styrofoam	_____%	Tins	_____%
Metal	_____%	Paper	_____%
Cardboard	_____%		

If you've answered 100 percent on each, I'm impressed! You got me beat.

76- There are the things we can choose to recycle that often we don't think of. There are many organizations that will take your old clothes, furniture and either dispose of or re-sell.

What percentage of the time do you donate the following items?

Clothing that you don't wear	_____%
Toys your kids don't use	_____%
Children's clothing	_____%
Furniture you don't want	_____%
Kitchen stuff-dishes, pots, appliances	_____%
Blankets/bedding	_____%
Food to a food bank or shelter	_____%
Old eyeglasses you aren't wearing	_____%
Vehicles	_____%

77-So many things we can do to help out one another. There is always someone less fortunate who gives life to what we no longer need. Speaking of donating with all the programs available I'm going to ask the following

What are the most advertised charity programs in your area for each of the following? Write their names down.

Medical fundraising _____

Shelter program _____

Feeding the homeless _____

Children's charity _____

Senior's charity _____

Clothing drives _____

78-Now along with charities there are the celebrities we hear of who make a stand and really help out. So in your opinion, whom do you believe assists charities the most? Top 3 that you believe have done the most.

_____

_____

_____

79-Back in question (27) we asked which company came first to mind when you needed something specific. These were companies that popped into your head automatically because their advertising just gets stuck there. So let's do some more. (Remember, don't think too long, just the first name that pops into your head)

Carpet cleaning: _____

Need justice call: _____

Thinking of home decorating: _____

Need new window coverings: _____

New living room furniture: _____

Computer problems: _____

Need a new car: _____

80- We looked at shopping in a grocery store and now we'll focus on those department stores. They are giant places with so many aisles, products and truly a vast array of goods available in a one stop shopping experience. Some are for clothing, while some now offer grocery as well.

Your favorite department store is _____

You shop there at least _____ times a month.

Your favorite department to visit is the _____ department.

Let's find out why it's your favorite. On a scale from 1-10, rate how you feel about each of the following in that store: (1 being the best of course)

Selection	_____	Customer service department	_____
Prices of goods	_____	It is organized	_____
It is clean	_____	Size of the aisles	_____
Clearly marked prices	_____	Offers a lot of sale items	_____
Has friendly sales staff	_____	Line-ups at the cashiers	_____
Really is one stop shopping	_____	Finding parking	_____
Carts available (good one's)	_____		

81- Well with the good, there is always the bad. So a few questions about the store you just don't like to ever have to walk into.

The one you hate going to the most is _____

Ok we're going to rate them, on all the same points. Even though they are not your favorite, we are going to figure out why you hate being in there. Be honest…I'm sure they have weak and strong points.

Selection	_____	Customer service department	_____
Prices of goods	_____	It is organized	_____
It is clean	_____	Size of the aisles	_____
Clearly marked prices	_____	Offers a lot of sale items	_____
Has friendly sales staff	_____	Line-ups at the cashiers	_____
Really is one stop shopping	_____	Finding parking	_____
Carts available (good one's)	_____		

82- Lately the service industry just ain't what it used to be, it could be just me, but more often than not I don't find friendly service and helpful assistance. Now those people have to deal with people all day long and I'm sure it gets tiresome, but they're hired for that purpose, right?

Whew! Now that I got that off my chest, how do you feel about this entire industry? Think about all the places you've been and rate them **A,B,C,D**, and that big fat **F** for failure, just like in school.

We are going to have a few options here just to help narrow things down a bit. But this is not about the product they sell, just the polite, courteous service they are supposed to provide. We're going to ask you to rate the industry overall compared to how it was way back when, then write the names of the company where you have experienced the best and the worst.

Fast Food restaurants:

    In general you find the service: _____ (A-F)

    The best service would be at: _____

    The worst would be at: _____

Service/Gas stations:

    In general the attendant service is: _____(A-F)

    The best service would be at: _____

    The worst is at: _____

Department Stores-those big national conglomerates:

    In general you find the service: _____ (A-F)

    The best service would be at: _____

    The worst service is at: _____

Movie theatres, there are several different chains:

    In general you find the service: _____(A-F)

    The best service would be at: _____

    The worst service is at: _____

Restaurants-the big chains for a sit down meal:

    In general you find the service: _____(A-F)

    The best service would be at: _____

    The worst service is at: _____

Government offices-we all have to go there at times.

    In general you find the service: _____(A-F)

    The best service would be at: _____

    The worst service is at: _____

83- We get to interact with people every day and it seems being polite and courteous is the way of the past. I try to think of why this would've happened. We are supposed to progress as the human race yet it seems the world is getting colder. I wonder what you think is going on? Can you give 5 one-word responses as to why people are so unapproachable?

_____   _____   _____

_____   _____

84- Just doesn't seem right-we have technology advancing us to new and exciting things yet we can't get a handle on simple kindness. We will ask you a few questions about how you are when you're out and about. Now this is when dealing with people you don't know, but see every day while out shopping or at work.

You say please/thank you _____ % of the time

You hold doors open for others _____ % of the time

You have deliberately closed the elevator while someone asked you to hold it open #_____ of times.

You put away things in the store where they came from if you decide you don't want it _____ % of the time.

You are careful to re-hang the clothes after trying them on in the change rooms and hand them back as neatly as you got them _____ % of the time.

You make a point of smiling at others in the store _____ % of the time.

You've allowed someone to go ahead of you at a cashier seeing they have only a few things compared to your full cart _____ % of time.

You assist elderly people putting bags in their car and struggling _____ % of the time.

You make small talk with others in a cashier line _____ % of the time.

You take the time to say good morning to those you work with at least _____ days a week.

You ask people how their day is going _____ % of the time.

You allow people to cut in while driving/merging _____ % of the time.

How'd you do? I wonder if we all took that few extra seconds to extend the hand of kindness....?

85-Back to the advertising in the world! Open a magazine and you'll see many different advertisements. I don't recognize a lot of the models or people used to spark our interest-I don't keep up with that stuff. We do have model reality shows yet I truly couldn't tell you who is who in the model world.

You would say the most well-known models in magazines are:

Female: _____

Male: _____

The most well-known model on television would have to be:

Female: _____

Male: _____

The most well-known Super Model is:

Female: _____

Male: _____

86-Many of those who start in modeling end up in the movies now gaining an acting career. Seems once they start they have opportunities all over the place. Some even have a singing career. (I'm starting to think I'm in the wrong job!). I can clearly remember some who transitioned from one to the other. Some I thought made great actors/actresses while some I thought stick to what you know.

Name 5 people who started as models then shifted to acting or singing-even if they just did it once

1 _____

2 _____

3 _____

4 _____

5 _____

Now from those 5 that you chose, rate each how well you think they did in all their careers. Again we will use the **A,B,C,D**, and that big old **F**.

	Modeling	Acting	Singing
1-	_____	_____	_____
2-	_____	_____	_____
3-	_____	_____	_____
4-	_____	_____	_____
5-	_____	_____	_____

87- Well no matter how they did they're making more than you or I will. I can't even imagine the paycheck for some of those folks. And with advertisers, I often wonder if celebrities get the products for free as well? I mean if they advertise a car, is that part of the contract? I could use a new vehicle, perhaps I'll offer my services!

If you could advertise any one product and be able to keep the product-now think carefully-could be a cruise, trip or innovative gadget-what would you like to advertise

_____

I wonder just how far you'd go to get that product…let's say they told you the commercial was filmed with you in the buff (naked), would you still do it?

_____ yes _____ no.

88-Funny the things we'll do sometimes to get something new and exciting. You see those people every day on TV who get their 15 minutes of fame, doing something totally off the wall. I just shake my head and wonder, why? Usually they're on your local newscast, that person who streaked across a field or is jumping up and down in the background. Yikes!

Have you had your 15 minutes of fame yet? _____ yes _____ no

If you have ever appeared on TV, even if it was in the background please do share that moment:

_____

_____

I don't think I've ever had the opportunity, well not yet anyways, with my luck it'll be something totally embarrassing so best not to go there.

89-Hey, we haven't even asked about talk shows! There are a zillion of them. Ok well maybe not a zillion…but there are lots. They have daytime, evening and late night talk shows ranging from political, sports, entertainment, news…and everything in between.

So let's ask what your favorites are at each time of the day:

Daytime talk show _____

Evening talk show _____

Late night talk show _____

Now with some of these show's I like the topics, yet I don't like the host. Some rattle on and on, with their opinions, or make one funny and then go on and on about it-yet the humor is lost.

Who do you think shouldn't be a talk show host _____

Who do you think needs new material _____

One of the best things about these types of shows is they interview people and we get to see just a bit more about our favorites. I would much prefer if ordinary people got to ask some of the questions because after all we put them in that chair by supporting their career.

So if you were allowed to write the script for all interviews of the Stars-what top 5 questions would you always ask?

1 _____

2 _____

3 _____

4 _____

5 _____

90-Time to have fun making our own commercials again! There are just too many to have fun with so it's hard to stop thinking about if we were at the helm, deciding what goes on television.

A-Sweepers that are supposed to make cleaning a breeze, there are several different kinds. They sure have some strange commercials for them. One commercial they have mops/brooms being rejected whilst love songs play in the background. Cute, but I'd much prefer to see them walking into a normal house where muddy footprints happened to dry. Yep, seems that kind of stuff happens and you catch it way after the fact.

You'd like to see a sweeper commercial:

_____

_____

_____

B-Laundry detergent commercials! Now there's a subject. Ever see those one's where kids jump in puddles or play in the muck and jump around on beds and stuff with muddy shoes? Now I don't know about your Mom, but if I ever did that, there would be no happy smiles and don't worry it'll come out talk. I'm actually trying to picture Mom's face if I would've ever done that. Yikes!

You'd like to see a laundry detergent commercial:

_____

_____

_____

C-Fast food commercials, ever notice how fresh it all looks on the commercial yet when you actually go get it-nope, not quite looking the same, it's usually all floppy, soggy and squished. Never looks like it's supposed to in my opinion.

You'd like to see your fast food commercial:

_____

_____

_____

D) What about those electronics/furniture store commercials? Most show the big sales of the week yet when you get to the store, usually you find they are all sold out of that offer. Hate when that happens, wastes my time driving down there for nothing.

You'd like to see those sales commercials:

_____

_____

_____

91-With the world of technology there are so many new gadgets for home security. You've probably seen them advertised all over the place. Home alarms, cameras, monitored alarms etc… Yep, seems its way important these days to have one.

Do you have a home security system　　　　_____yes _____no

Do you have the camera system too　　　　　_____yes _____no

How often has it gone off so far by mistake _____

On a scale from 1-10, it's how loud   _____

Have you got one for your vehicle too   _____ yes _____ no

Have you ever been broken into   _____ yes _____ no

Has your car been broken into   _____ yes _____ no

My neighbors had a group of kids come into their yard in broad daylight and pull a snowmobile trailer with two sleds on it by hand. Everyone saw them! You gotta wonder what's this world is coming to, where are their parents is my question? Yep they wired up their whole yard.

92-Now some of the commercials that just get to me every time are the ones for animal shelters and abused animals. They truly are heart touching. It's sad to think this goes on in today's world. You know the one's I mean, when you see battered, terrified animals, being rescued. That is advertising that should make people stop and think twice. There are other commercials as well that just touch your heart-almost make you cry. All those touching on Cancer, Alzheimer's, Heart Disease…human frailty, truly are heart touching advertising.

What top 3 commercials really get to you?

_____

_____

_____

Do you belong to any charitable organizations? If you're not a member, but have contributed to a few along the way, please list them:

_____

_____

_____

_____

93-I often wonder about the advertising world. Of course we all know it is to sell products and services, yet at times I wonder just how much we end up buying that we really didn't need, times are tough nowadays so money is best invested in necessities.

Overall you would say you buy things _____% of the time that you really didn't need and only purchased due to the hype.

You would say that _____% of your purchases are necessary in sustaining life day to day.

You would say that _____% of the time you end up regretting purchasing something that you don't really use as much as you thought you would.

94-Seems years ago cleaners would be home made with combinations of vinegar, baking soda, ammonia, lemons etc…and it was enough to keep our homes clean. There were various recipes for different uses. If you were to check under your kitchen sink or into that cleaner cupboard, how many different bottles of prefab cleaners are there?

You would guess that you have _____ different bottles of cleaners in your home.

Once you've entered a guess, go around and check all cupboards, closets and add them up.

Actual count is _____

I was watching a show recently about flesh eating bacteria-a virus that runs rampant through our system and becomes fatal. The doctor on the show stated that with constantly using anti-bacterial soaps and cleaners…we are killing off bacteria we need to strengthen our immune system. It was quite an eye opener. I guess it makes sense-we need bacteria to kill off bacteria. Maybe our forefathers had it right with keeping it simple. Something to think about!

95-These last 5 questions I'm going to turn things a bit more towards how you feel about it all. You've had a chance to laugh, have fun and reflect on advertising in this world.

So looking around your world right now, you can honestly say that you are most grateful for advertising bringing what into your life?

_____

Looking at your family's needs and wants, they all get affected by what they see and hear. For some it is the name brands and wanting top of the line, others it's just the advertising they see every day stuff.

In these hard times, it sometimes is hard to not provide all that we wish we could. So on that note, you wish advertising would stop showing what product or service to your family since you can't afford it:

_____

96- Without the world of advertising, I suppose we wouldn't learn of new products to enhance life. Heck I'm single, so I would never have known that Viagra may help my future spouse if it weren't for commercials. (I'll probably be elderly by the time I meet Mr. Right-so it's good to know.)

What one product/service taught you something you didn't know or enhanced your life ten-fold

_____

97- With technology it seems we want everything in an instant these days and for what we don't see on TV, we can now use the internet and find anything with a little research. The information highway

You have how many computers in your family_____

Do you monitor what sites are used _____% of the time

Your biggest complaint about the technology of internet

_____

_____

The best thing about it is

_____

_____

98-Back in question 82-about the service industry, we asked about how you felt about it all. Those people who are supposed to be there for us with kind, courteous, helpful service. So we're going to look at just a few more industries here. Again think about all the places you've been, and rate them **A,B,C,D**, and that big fat **F** for failure.

Remember, rate the industry overall, then write the names, of the company where you have experienced the best and the worst.

Grocery stores-first the large chains that spread across the nation:

    In general you find the service: _____

    The best service would be at: _____

    The worst would be at: _____

Now the small Mom and Pop stores local to you:

    In general you find the service: _____

    The best service would be at: _____

    The worst would be at: _____

Parks, recreating or theme-where you at times take your children:

    In general you find the service: _____

    The best service would be at: _____

    The worst would be at: _____

99-Is service what it used to be? I can't really say for anyone but myself. We all have opinions and I wonder if we were to ask questions of ourselves on our ability to be kind, courteous and always helpful…how well would we do? Not all of us take the time to understand, wait, be patient and put our best foot forward. When we're out shopping, traveling for work or running our errands

Myself, my family, are sure to be polite and kind at least what percent of the time?

IN:

Grocery stores	_____%
Retail stores	_____%
At service stations	_____%
At the movies	_____%
At a restaurant	_____%
At a park	_____%
When dealing with officials	_____%
At work or school	_____%

100-Wow! 100 Questions, I bet you thought you'd never get through it all. Every day we have the opportunity to reach out to someone. Every day we get the chance to take that extra moment to make the world a kinder place. With the hustle and bustle world we live in, at times we don't stop to think about that. It's all about the rat-race of work, home, money, we want, we want, we want! I guess it is how we're evolving and the bottom-line is what we focus on. It is my hope that we get back to times when people weren't a number and we don't wait until they're gone to remember their value to our lives. With the commercial world they fill our heads with what is needed and what we should want in life.

Beauty is not some picture in a magazine and wealth is not the bling you can show off. Not in my opinion anyways, it is the grace to accept oneself and others, no matter of circumstance…to reach out with kindness and understanding. To live comfortably and never forget we are all equals. We are all born and we all will die, what we do in between those times is what truly matters. That's the true wealth in life, we are all someone's daughter, brother, mother, father, sister and friend. We all matter!

For this question, I'd like you to answer how you feel about the whole world of money and what society/advertising tries to sell us. You've had a chance to really laugh and look at all that transpires in your world.

You believe that society says we have to:

_____

You believe that we can make this world a better place by:

_____

You feel that advertising should spend more time selling us:

_____

I do hope you enjoyed going through this book and looking at your world through your eyes. There are more volumes in this series to help us stop for a moment and look at everything around us. Laugh, Live, Love and be proud.

Wendy Proteau

Blessed with three siblings and parents who supported my hopes, I was raised in a small Canadian town, in an average middle-class family. Single at age forty-something, I'm still figuring life out daily. Being a combination of realist and dreamer, you can only imagine the confusion that goes on internally. Half of me writes a story with 'the happily ever after', the other half, edits the work and keeps it more realistic.

I'd never written more than a grocery list until 2009. It came out of nowhere as I sat at my computer following an idea. The *'Sit N Do Nothing Hamster Series'* is my way to bring us all a little closer in this technological world. The workbooks of self-discovery are a way to share tidbits of who we are, in the here and now. Each of the seven volumes, designed for a specific audience, asks the reader about their lives. I have many more ideas to expand the series. This hamster never quits! They are now available via print on demand.

Finding my inner voice, I decided to try my hand at a fiction. *'And When'* was written from September 2010–January 2011. Receiving many reviews, the story resonated, often bringing them to tears, laughter, and at times… needing a cold towel.

Taking months to edit the final draft, I began to miss that creative energy and *'Now What'* the sequel was started in 2012 and published in 2013. The story continues to place difficult hurdles, forcing the characters to veer from their chosen paths.

My life would be nothing without the people who have touched my soul. Friends, family, co-workers, relatives…have all been there through the good and bad. Everything takes hard work and nothing ever comes easy. Well at least not in my life. I firmly believe that karma plays an important role. It brings us the people we are meant to meet, challenges we have to overcome, lessons we need to learn and dreams we are meant to reach for.

The Sit 'N' Do Nothing Hamster Series

Unlock Your Hamster-Volume One
An introduction to the series

The Single Man Hamster-Volume Two

The Single Woman Hamster-Volume Three

Hamsters Unite-The Relationship-Volume Four
Dating, Married or Living Together

Heart Broke Hamster-Volume Five
For the tough spots of break-up, divorce or loss

The Gotta Have Hamster-Volume Six
Advertising and what you buy into

The Hospital Hamster-Volume Seven
For those in hospital or home recuperating

www.wendiann.com